AFTER *the* AFTERLIFE

ALSO BY T. R. HUMMER

AFTER *the* AFTERLIFE

POEMS

T. R. HUMMER

ACRE

CINCINNATI 2017

Acre Books is made possible by the support of the Robert and Adele Schiff Foundation.

Designed by Barbara Neely Bourgoyne
Cover art: John Sokol, *Man Eating Christmas Trees*, altered postcard, 5 in. x 7 in.

Library of Congress Cataloging-in-Publication Data are available at the Library of Congress.
ISBN-10 (pbk): 1–946724–01–7 | ISBN-13 (pbk): 978–1-946724–01–4
ISBN-10 (ebook): 1-946724-06-8 | ISBN-13 (ebook): 978-1-946724-06-9

The press is based at the University of Cincinnati, Department of English and Comparative Literature, McMicken Hall, Room 248, PO Box 210069, Cincinnati, OH, 45221–0069. www.acre-books.com

Acre Books books may be purchased at a discount for educational use. For information please email business@acre-books.com.

I searched myself.

—HERACLITUS

For Theo, Victor, Beth, and Emma:
my phalanx

CONTENTS

I. DESERT

We circle in the night and are devoured by fire.

—HERACLITUS

FUGUE IN D MINUS

All those years while I sat in the desert mourning
    the blank staff of the sky and the dense
Score of the mountains on the edge of vision, I thought
    how the hummingbird darting before the ocotillo
Was transcribing a sonata by Scarlatti—how hard
    it worked, how effortless it seemed—
And how the falcon harvesting kangaroo mice cut
    with the incisive delicacy of a staccato harpsichord.
And so I failed Mysticism, and received a D- in Religion,
    because I could not let go of the music,
Anathema to inquisitors, acceptable to priests
    as a poor but necessary substitute, and understood
By the wisest ascetics as the horizonless sphere,
    empty as resignation, bloody and naked and pure.

FIRST PERSON

Today I wash a few dishes and scrub out the sink,
    then wander around in the yard, aimlessly
Pulling out a couple of weeds. Next, I go check
    the closet to see if my one dress shirt
Needs ironing. This is how I get ready for the funeral.
    For years I shunned the first person.
I was tired of saying *I*. Even to look at it there
    in italic would have made me a little dizzy.
But now I come back to it as I dust off my good shoes
    and consider my two neckties laid out
On the bed like a pair of Roman numerals. If I
    take one up, what will the other amount to? One
Abandoned pronoun putzing around in the world.

HOUSE

Not in houses, but rooms in cheap hotels
    or charity wards: so the great musicians died,
The ones who played jazz or blues. There was one,
    it is true, who did it on the sofa of a baroness
In Manhattan, in a penthouse suite, no less, but it belonged
    to that curious heiress, not to him. Leaking faucets
And ripped carpets were their destiny, wallpaper
    so lost it would take an Oscar Wilde to curse it.
It hurts my heart to think of them in the 50s, singing
    each other farewell through dumbwaiters
And moldy airshafts. I walk from room to room,
    the travertine floors are cool, I go barefoot
The better to feel them, I sit in a leather chair
    in front of an enormous sunny window,
Watching strangers plant a garish yellow sign
    beside the walk. I hum "A House is Not a Home."
I can't remember the words. I hear Bill Evans play it
    on *I Will Say Goodbye*. 1977: he is riffing cocaine
In the third movement of the longest suicide in history.
    It is a worthy thing to sell a house. It is good to throw away
So much repression from garages and attics, right to take
    bags of clothes to Goodwill, straightening and lightening the load.
The Baroness comes into her parlor. When she left it,
    a genius was snoring "Now's the Time." And now
The silence in the room is an infinite caesura. She takes
    her shoes off to walk respectfully, she pulls the curtains,
Blocking out the oblivious insult of Fifth Avenue
    and Central Park, where the homeless
Are dying meaninglessly, their solitary music
    evaporating in moonlight, moving no one anywhere.

MY DAUGHTER'S PASSPORT

It is a tiny book, a cross section of a Gideon Bible
    or a pocket Kabbalah. It smells of amaryllis
And serotonin when I hold it to my nose and gnaw
    in worship. Portals to other dimensions are crystalline,
Diamantine, they show distorted tableaus
    of the nameless place, but you cannot pass,
Rat, you are forbidden. At fourteen, my daughter
    is a study in the purity of sweet alienation,
Surrounded by concertina wire and fiery customs officials
    and what looks, through my fogged telescope,
Like an ectoplasmic minefield. She studies the face
    of the armadillo, the profile of the hooded rat. I am
The rat. I was there in the beginning, when she crossed
    the border from concealment into the realm
Of the unconcealed. I held her documents in my clawed paw.
    I squealed until she saw me. She took what I offered,
She reached the gate, and was permitted. That is a life.
    This book of her face holds a record of her journey
In a golden tetragrammaton illegible to rodents.
    On the shelf of her psyche, the rabbit, the cow, the holy dog,
And the owl shake their heads in animal disgust
    that a rat should have a passport. Friends, it was never mine.
If it were, like her, I would be human. If it were, like her,
    I would hold my beauty close to my belly, I would weep
In dignified bliss, I would sail from one world to the next
    rich with solitude and language, bearing over
My heart in its bone crate safe from the rat in steerage,
    brilliant pilgrim, beloved plaything, destroyer of worlds.

RECOVERED LIVES

Wasn't I a German once, sailing my miserable boat
 in the North Sea, casting my nets for lobsters?
I remember the cold, I was always blue, I shivered
 like a dog with a seizure. Do I dredge this up
Out of the repressed memory of the reborn, or is it the genes
 having a little party and reminiscing? My name
In German means *lobster*, though the family history
 peters out at a brewery in Bavaria, a landlocked place
Where maybe I used my boat as a trough for pigs.
 My boat was my fate for many lives, that I know;
In Heligoland I rowed among the islands, avoiding Frisians
 for their lechery and Danes for their endless conversation.
Nights the stars froze and floated down disguised as snow,
 and my boat and I wandered from island to island, only
Hoping for a little fire and a bowl of chowder, but the locals concocted
 fish soups of such vileness even my boat's heart sank.
It was a long time before it occurred to me I could love anything,
 the sea of my genealogy was so relentless, studded
With such obdurate stone. I lived and died without noticing
 much of a difference. Even the lobsters were cannibals,
So my name devoured my name and spat itself out again.
 Now in another country the blood moon hangs itself
Over the peaceful village, and my patient wife reminds me
 I no longer need a net, and lobsters are out of season,
Which is code for the purity of happiness in our peaceful life,
 and we sleep entwined under blankets spread in the frame of a boat,
Which is what Odysseus should have done at the end of the story
 instead of walking to Germany, carrying his useless oar.

IN A SMALL PARK WITH BENCH,
JACARANDA, AND BIRD'S SKULL

A woman was praying for a clump of fern to sprout
    or otherwise make a miraculous appearance on the ground
Beside her, to soften the harsh linearity of the concrete bench
    she had chosen to sit on, or that had chosen to be under her,
But she was sure she was not one of the chosen, for if she were,
    a fern would emerge wherever she commanded,
And she needed it also because she objected to the jacaranda,
    which was at the peak of its bloom: it was so atmospheric
In its lavender hubris that it threatened to drag her back
    into a childhood that didn't bear repeating.
Instead it so happened that a boy ran up from the playground,
    set the skull of a bird on her knee, and dashed away coughing
Like a terminal consumption victim—the child could be forgiven,
    he had short-circuited the terrible vortex of her early life
With the vacuum of his own, and the talisman he had brought
    was the skull of a grackle, picked clean by ants and burnished
Through a season of dust and a season of plague, and when she picked it up,
    it seemed to her she could hear the echo of a distant flock
Of others all alike who could conceal her in their identical natures
    so that never again would she suffer alone the curse of selfhood, the famine
Of melancholia, the ache of the tremendum, what it means to live a life
    in a city in the heartland beside a mill that stinks like the corpse of God.

IN UTAH

I used to go out before sunup in February, breasting the vicious
    wind that came down from the High Uintas—
Such cold that I grew a beard to protect me, and prayed
    to the Mormon ravens to enfold me in their ragged nests—
Laboring up the foothill along East 100th Street, from the flat
    where I lived underground like a character from Dostoyevsky
To the Abattoir of Knowledge where I taught poetry to the young
    who desired to partake of metrics at seven in the morning
Before they were sent the world over carrying Truth and Beauty
    to people in Tonga, etc.—was I complicit in that, since I read them Keats?
So many young men in neckties, beardless, assembled in the classroom's
    natural supernatural darkness, waiting to learn metaphor and rhyme,
That in my confusion I studied again *The Book of Enoch* to learn
    how angels behave when they come among us, I turned
Once more to Swedenborg and Blake. But the young men grew restive
    when I spent three classes reading *Jerusalem* aloud,
They refused to write 500 lines of visionary strophes,
    they complained to the Dean of Cattle, and I was reprimanded,
And returned to ordinary poets: Snyder and Brooks and Stern,
    wheezing uphill in the razored wind with a raven on my shoulder
To protect me from anarchists, pit bulls, motorbikes, and Bible salesmen,
    believing nothing in the nest of my soul that could not be enjambed,
And I came each day to the Abattoir and took up the hammer again
    to crush the skull of each animal in turn, but precisely and tenderly.

IMPERVIOUS BLUE

We walked down Main Street past the barber shop
    where men's heads hovered over tents of stained cloth,
Past the pharmacy, outside of which stood a marvelous machine
    that would weigh you and tell you the future if you dropped
A penny in—and how I wanted to pull the lever and receive the news
    of futures that seemed inevitable: I would be homeless in winter,
Naked in an empty steel boxcar crusted with permafrost, or, shipwrecked
    and pursued by rabid monkeys, fall into a pit of spiders. But my father
Refused, my future was not worth a penny, and we walked on
    past benches where black men in overalls sat talking quietly,
Watching us with tired eyes as we went past, their hands hard
    from cotton bolls and wrenches, their work boots ruptured. 1957:
There were futures no machine could fathom on the edge of their vision
    in Mississippi, not even the one in the store where we went to buy
New shoes: where I stared through the scope at the ghost of my own toes,
    my precious white bones ghosted in x-ray far below me
Through a wormhole of darkness wherein I could see a city burning,
    pistols cracking skulls, children bleeding, and I was one of them,
Thrown to a curb in Chicago, Birmingham, Memphis, unconscious
    then as now, my shoeless feet bruised from white to impervious blue.

EVERYDAY METAPHYSICS

The memory of being born is the memory of dying
    and memory is a notorious liar. It's a Monday in October
If memory serves, though I sometimes think it's a Friday,
    so how can I think about where I was last Tuesday,
Much less before I was born? And being dead? Forget it.
    That's what we do, except when we don't.
To Calvinists, death is all about discipline and punishment,
    as if their game plan were written by Michel Foucault.
I heard a famous Buddhist say that sentient life extends
    through the whole expanse of space and time
And that in the course of eternity every sentient thing
    has been the father, mother, and devourer of every other.
I take that as a description of samsāra, that scum
    of illusion within which I feed the cat, pay my taxes
And do my laundry, as I am doing now. Chop wood, carry water.
    The journey from washer to drier is a crisis, especially for the socks,
Who continually lose their sole-mates. This particular one,
    black with tiny spots like a cloud of stars, I have washed
Solo maybe a dozen times, so great is its mourning,
    so sublime its hope that if it goes through every cycle
It will come back to where it began, and begin, no longer alone.

GLASS CEILING

Because she wanted to teach me a lesson
    about the natural world, my grandmother raised
Her .22 rifle—we were rabbit hunting, so the shotgun
    was at home under her blue chintz pillow—and brought
A quail down on the covey rise. Impossible shot
    you may be thinking. True. I said "my grandmother"
Because if I'd said "my mother" you wouldn't believe
    a word of it, since a mother should be leading
A research group, or running a software company,
    but a grandmother still can dress in buckskin
And ride a fabulous palomino, doing handstands
    on the saddle, executing trick shots blindfold
With a musket, reloading on the fly, while deep
    in the underbrush I gather the rabbits to me
And we tremble together in the riptide of her passing.

DOVE

A pestilence of doves descends, an idiocy
    of fowl, sister of the pigeon, comrade
Of the seagull and all rats with wings. The lawn
    is seeded with cereal of a noxious kind
Bought for a child and left too long uneaten.
    I was hoping for quail, or sparrows at least,
Maybe a western grackle, birds of dignity
    and character, or maybe a sense of humor—
The grackle will do stand-up, or imitate
    a jackhammer. But the mourning dove
Is a stomach with legs, it is dull of plumage
    and stupid. Its flock is a judgment against me.
I remember that if the offering to the Lord
    is a burnt offering, you are to offer up
A dove, or a young pigeon. I remember he waited
    seven more days and again sent out the dove
From the ark. My dove in the clefts of the rock
    and the hiding places on the mountainside,
Forgive me my failures. I asked for a slapstick grackle,
    I was given a squab in blackface. They will come
Trembling like birds from Egypt, like doves
    from Assyria. I have scattered my manna,
My sacrifice is refused. Soon this house
    and everything it holds will vanish, all these chattels,
A great wind will rage across the desert and strike
    its four corners down. The doves waddle strangely
Like stunted ducks in anticipation. It is March
    the eleventh in the provinces of the Milky Way.
The dove, the swift, and the thrush observe the time
    of their migration. I will honor mine, in my fashion.

I will strike my tent and begin my fated divagation
    over the quantum veldts and labyrinths to my love.
Show me your face, let me hear your voice, deliverance.
    Dreaming of grackles, I am left in the dust with my dove.

PREHISTORIC

Of the time before I could speak, I cannot speak.
    I was prehistoric, doing the dinosaur lurch
Across my crib. The world was there, worlding away,
    and I was in it, being worlded. Now I mourn
Everything between my birth and the first word I spoke,
    that skeletal man hacking arrowheads out of the black holes
Of obsidian cliffs, that woman grappling trout and water snakes
    over and over from the same impossible river. Elephants
Evolved heavily, ants built stadiums where people were gathered
    and shot. When the first utterance crossed my teeth's barrier,
The world lit up like a pinball machine, cause and effect caroming
    off meaning—I know because this I am forced to remember.
My parents put on clothes, animals marched through barbed-wire gates
    into fields of taxonomy, and I became the librarian of my own
Mechanical logos: human, shelved and numbered in the stacks
    of interiority, barricaded, sealed with intricate locks, recorded
And copied in triplicate by holy scriveners sacrificed at every sunrise,
    while beyond, the world mourned like all the mundane forgotten,
Vacant, fertile, pure, and flowing forward, speechless with loneliness.

HERACLITUS

After I learned to read I became hermetic,
    wrestling at six with names like Bumppo
And Nemo, who weren't Marx Brothers—them
        I knew firsthand from the black cube of the RCA
My father installed in the corner. After I learned
        to read, I scaled my cloven brain in crystal,
I moved on from pure orality, I no longer climbed
        into the black limbs of the ancient cedar
To croak back the gossip of crows. While cotton gins
        pounded in the distance and tractors groaned
All night in fields of the family desperation, pooling
        light around their furious bodies to finish
Writing our story in the earth, I murdered Kipling,
        I strangled the wonderful wizard, I ate Ishmael.
Who did I think I was to abandon singing
        what the bees were thinking, how did I lose
My voice? When I failed to understand Brontë,
        why did I mislay my daemon the Logos,
Why did my thoughts turn into bad dialogue
        from pulp science fiction? Always before,
I would meet Heraclitus on the footbridge
        in the forest, he would straighten my toga
And tell me how to memorize fire, how to become
        an egret or an ant. But when I read Plato, Heraclitus
Vanished, and the wind stopped stoking my larynx,
        I became a millstone rotated at a distance
By the power of the river, but never gazing into the water
        where quicksilver minnows were being forever
Devoured by the turtle lodged in the gut of the world.

DIDACTIC

The interior voice, the monkey mind, is tireless,
    nattering literally like mad, or metaphorically
Like a distant cousin I met once when I was twelve,
    who corners me now at the funeral with a litany
Of imaginary ills and a pointless story about Grandfather,
    who drank himself to dust because *his* grandfather
Was a trader of slaves. When you read a book, you upload
    another member of the family, like that moment
In chapter one of a Zane Grey novel when I was seven,
    the pioneer couple I had just begun to like, murdered
Before my tender eyes by inhuman redskins, not even
    a capital R, as if I weren't already racist enough
Just from the things my parents told me, their judging
    sermons I can't get rid of it, the auctioneer's jeering
Chant, the whip's economic report, plus the voice now screaming
    No! Not the nice white pioneers! It was all done to teach
A lesson about consciousness, how it needs to dream it has
    a center, a core, an essence, which is like trying to teach
The cat to waltz, so much awkwardness, so many tender
    advances, and I'm shocked when it actually learns,
When it minces toward me in a tiny cocktail gown, offering a martini,
    asking for this dance, insisting on hearing me refuse
To reply, debating all along, in the chorus of its interior mewing, who
    are you really, peculiar animal, who taught you to call you *you*.

THE MORNING MAIL

The condition of man...is a condition of war of everyone against everyone.
    —THOMAS HOBBES

If the cells of the toenail and the cells of the heart speak
        in the same voice, what is the body
Saying? This morning the sun comes in so strong
        I have to squint to read about the Leviathan,
Because there is unease in the kneecap, there is a stiff
        wind blowing through the appendix, and I know
That the whole *Common-Wealth Ecclesiasticall and Civill*
        is muttering its malaise in the noise of the garbage truck
And the obsessive-compulsive braying of a car alarm
        down the block. The cat in my lap is in an ecstasy
Of laziness, I can feel her deep purr in my thighs,
        and though she lies against me so intensely
It is as if she wants to melt into my body, she is not
        my body, she is her own Leviathan, she has a hunger
In her belly that I lack, she has an ecstasy I can only imagine,
        the multitude of her fur is a rabble marching on the Capitol.
The flesh of the body politic is a baby in a stroller at Walmart,
        and an ancient woman with a walker who once
Was a concert pianist, and the man who carries a pouch
        of cheap newsprint from mailbox to mailbox
Because there's no such thing anymore as a first-class letter.
        Conscience is what we know together. Look up the roots
Of the word. Look down the street at the vacant lot.
        Look down the Leviathan's maw. Its unbearable roar
Is the carrier wave of what we do this morning, what we have
        for breakfast, and shall I shave or go another day
A shade more disreputably? I should write someone an epistle
        with a quill pen on parchment. I should draw a dragon

18

In the margin and scent it with myrrh and motor oil.

   The mailman needs a *raison d'être*, not much, but it's a living
Going back and forth all day, sewing the body together.

   They buried Thomas Hobbes in St. John the Baptist
Churchyard, Derbyshire, and there the cells of the hand

      he wrote with still agitate and mutter, a vague
Chatter of bone-dust, the folly of a ribcage, bitterness of skull.

   The resurrection of the body is political. They're voting
In the provinces. Écrasez l'infâme. They're saying *no*.

   O Hobbes, don't bother getting up, nobody loves you.
Even the cat growls in her sleep, brutish, short, and dull.

WOLF

There is angst, which is a philosophical luxury,
    and there is anxiety, which is a black wolf.
It wants to rip you open to eat your liver. You can try
    to make friends, but it remains an animal,
Starving and sidelong. I first encountered him
    in an office, where you wouldn't think wolves
Would enter, but he came in dressed as a bureaucrat
    with a dossier of papers, one of which
Appeared to be a contract, but I wasn't asked
    for my soul, I was to give up my grandmother—
Wolves are death on those—who was the one person
    in my childhood who could calm me.
She would dress in black, take her walking stick,
    and go out into the orchard, where dark birds—crows?—
Were blitzing the harvest. She'd raise her cane
    skyward, and they'd vanish. How could I relinquish her?
I refused to sign. My punishment was this wolf
    who goes with me everywhere, opening doors
For the elderly, comforting crying children, reciting
    poems, and all the while waiting for me
To weaken, to slip, to fall asleep, and then he'll chain me
    to a cliff like my brother, angst-riddled Prometheus—
Those incompetent birds weren't crows, they were bloody eagles—
    and, efficient as only a wolf can be, finally finish the job.
Fear is a thing of the body, fear of the body is a thing
    only wolves are immune to—and bureaucrats, their avatars.

KERF

The rain in this desert valley is desperate and ugly,
    it does not so much fall as collapse
Like a throat-cut hostage. It brings down dust
    and the flatulence of jets, it brings down angst
And terminal loneliness, nurturing
    rattlesnakes and roadkill. Houses fill
With a peculiar yellow light. It reminds me
    of a bus ride from Tulsa to Lolo, Montana,
When I sat next to a stranger who wept silently
    over the Great Plains, and after hours,
The jagged kerf of the Rockies bloody
    under a dull sunset, she fell asleep
And went on crying. What is the name
    of the thirst that followed her
Into her private darkness all those years ago?
    If I walk outside and tip my head toward
The bleary sky, the slit of my mouth unhealed, I will fill
    with the drizzling rasp of her breathing again.

ARCHITECT

How nice it would be to die swimming into the sun,
      Le Corbusier said more than once, in French,
Wherein the word *nice* is nicer. Why would you want to live
      in such an ugly building—live, or work, or pray,
Or stand in an endless queue for a copy of your death certificate?
      The sun draws its fiery line across the Mediterranean,
Italicizing Europe. Who dares to cross the great water
      while children cling to their rubber swans, dabbling
In the shallows, and the old man sits sipping his negroni?
      The shade of a striped umbrella bruises the blueprints
Of the blitzkrieg, rolled up and tossed on the sand
      next to his towel and sandals. But you: enter here. Line up.
The hallway is pleasant, by design. It is hung with paintings
      of nothing. It ends in a burning portal. *How nice it would be.*

MINUTIAE

I never underestimate the housefly, its micro-mechanism
     buzzed with vinegar and honey, its hairy guts
Splattered on the kitchen window. I pay homage likewise
     to the spider and the woodlouse, the emperor moth
And the wasp. All these souls precede us. Where would I be
     without the carpenter ant and the exalted one, the scarab?
To live side by side on the earth is to suck one another dry.
     I stand at the kitchen sink at twilight clipping
My fingernails into running water, not in fear of witchcraft
     but of the Board of Health, if they inspected private homes.
In my gut (as in yours, Cleopatra, my Empress, my Queen) a horde
     of silent germs labor over my recent dinner, processing,
Waging holy war. *God is eternal surfeit*, Heraclitus whispers.
     I have grown too old to dream of whispering, and the grackles
Disdain to weep like their weakling cousin robins,
     and the leaves and the moon have dissolved
Like vinyl records under acid rain in that cardboard box
     I left in a leaky storeroom behind a house I lived in
Thirty years ago, full of rat pellets and moldy fertilizer sacks
     and a tintype of a woman who died a year before
The Civil War: she is playing a parlor guitar
     and maybe humming, she is calcium dust and wax,
A doll with my face, bristling with needles, bearing the secret
     of her life like forgotten music gutting the twilight, vanished now
Into bacteria and potash and a soul particulate as galaxies.

FISHER CAT

Dead center in my insomnia her interior scream
    crowns in her throat, and the bedroom dissolves.
As deep in woods as the amygdala in the brain, the fisher cat
    is God's pure sentience of terror. Through her
God is instructed in freeze and leap and rip, for every atom
    of her creation is bonded with fear. Not cat but weasel, she
Is the avatar of adrenalin and cortisol. In her lair, she is asleep,
    her head toward the portal, her dreaming eyes are open.
For holy horror of you, Lord, she will claw vision from your skull.
    Live in her. You will learn quiver, crouch, and lunge,
You will vibrate with her voice, which is a refuge and a weapon.
    This is why you made her. Go to her. I will pray for you, Lord.
Even from the core of her nightmare, she is eternally aware of you.

SKY BURIAL

A bed knocked apart with a hammer—no,
    not the mattress, the bed: a simple platform
Cunningly wrought of particle board and fastened
    with pot metal and frankincense. Mine weapon
A bludgeon like a Nietzsche aphorism, I unmade it
    in minutes, each gargantuan blow an insult
To the history of optimism. It was a bed from another world
    my daughter slept in nightly those few nights
She spent still in this fortress. How she wandered
    the dusty marble halls, how the empty armor
Refused to sing to her under the balustrade. And now
    the armies of *ressentiment* have murdered God
And the tree in the courtyard withers. For this
    old warrior, there is only the warless war,
So I beat apart the bed I made with my wasting
    hands when, in the beginning, there was light
And it had a constant speed, and a sun to leak it, and a sky
    to hold it. I shore the sulfurous fragments
By the curb for bulk-trash pickup and strap my wrists
    to the wreck, waiting for the clash of gears and the great
White vultures of suburbia, here in the Land of Alikeness,
    to circle, whetting their carrion beaks, wanting to pick me
Slick, bone by alabaster, under the obsidian dome: O
    make me clean for the new life, Masters, break me whole.

II. RIVER

Death, to the soul, is to become as water.
—HERACLITUS

WATER

The water is not the shape pressed on the tense meniscus
    by wind, nor the scene revealed beneath it
Wherein the constant thrash of fish distracts me
    from the stillness of the drowned child
And my own shadow staring up through her eyes.
    Somewhere in between, the water hovers—
Undefinable, older than pain, mindful in its absence
    of my presence, I who remember
The child I was, how I desired, how I went under.

MY VOICE

It is an instrument not unlike the sackbut,
    odd, but less ancient than is generally thought,
Useful for hailing cabs and torturing cats.
    And though the sackbut is biblical,
We are not talking about the biblical sackbut,
    since that instrument was a Syrian lute,
And this is a small trombone, not tiny enough
    to fit in my pocket, but not so enormous
That I can't easily haul it along to a picnic
    or to an Indian restaurant, where it is regarded
As an unclean thing. Its metal is bright but not precious—
    reflective, so that when I look at it, I see
A warped version of my face, as in a saddle mirror.
    Mornings I take it out of its case and run through
My repertoire of scales, exercises, and etudes.
    It reminds me it is an avatar of the Logos,
But it is not biblical, because it does not summon
    the people to worship any graven image.
I work tenderly with it to master a riff of Jack Teagarden's,
    not at all the kind of thing that brought down Jericho,
Those were trumpets, if memory serves, and if memory
    doesn't serve, then what the hell good is it? My voice
Is the voice of memory. I will someday forget it and leave it
    in the back of a Manhattan cab, perhaps, or, more majestically,
At a pawnshop in New Orleans, where some small child
    might see it, and wonder at it, and beg for it, until
Her father buys it for her, and in its seductive shimmer
    she will burn as I once did and learn what not to see.

AS FOR THE HOUSEFLY

Bashing its head against the kitchen window,
    its sentience is a quasar, it has lived
Twenty fly years trying to understand transparency,
    while for me, only half a day has passed
Since it blew in the back door as I was getting the mail.
    But I hear the cosmos howling fiercely inside
Its minuscule cranium. Time is compressed in its soul
    like neutrons in plasma. When I walk
Across the kitchen, I am continental drift, I move
    my arms like a spiral galaxy. No wonder
It is frantic as I open the pane. How long must it take
    for the air to cool and the sun to sink into
Its consciousness, how long for the speed of light to change?

ANSEL ADAMS ON THE MOON

It's a question of contrast—the issue is middle gray,
    and just when you think you've metered it,
It nails you to the wall. If I look at enough of these photographs
    I get tired of Ansel Adams, bored with the way he thinks.
I hunger for something odd of Weston's, or give it up altogether
    and go back to a sublimely ugly burgher by Vermeer.
Adams worked so slowly for the lyric, his craft so absolutely conscious,
    that half his subjects died waiting for the shutter to fall,
And the other half gave up and looked for different work,
    or stood in line at a soup kitchen in Santa Fe, holding out
Their stony hands for menudo and a white tortilla scrap. But then
    I come across the moon, weightless over Hernandez,
New Mexico, still exactly the way it was that day it surprised him
    at 4:05 p.m. local time, October 31, 1941. It was Halloween,
Nine years before I was born. Adams says nothing of that.
    How could he leave out the American Day of the Dead?
How could he forget I was waiting to appear? He'd spent hours failing
    to satisfy himself with the stump of a cottonwood—it refused
To be imagined. And here was the moon as he'd never seen it.
    He had two minutes and thirty-seven seconds to capture it
Inside the massive 8×10 Deardorff before the scene eroded,
    no time even to meter, but he realized he knew the exact
Luminance, how much light the moon threw down (250 c/ft²),
    so he dialed it in and the world stood still. Down in the village, kids
Were dressing up as zombies and unborn poets. One wore my face and wove
    down the haunted avenues. I was still almost that boy's lifetime
From coming into focus, still nearly a decade from the aperture,
    but the moon rolled on against the film of the darkening sky,
While inside the camera's negative space—all because the Maestro knew
    his light—its soul waited to be dodged and burned.

PUB WITH MAGNIFICENT PANELING
AND TERRIBLE CHAIRS

She was there to meet an old friend who had not yet arrived,
    so to kill time she was looking around—she'd eavesdrop,
She thought, on the conversations of people much younger
    to see if mating rituals had changed since she had worshiped
At that altar—but she found herself unable to hear, the music
    was so loud and alien, and honestly her inner ear
Produced a constant high-pitched whine like a plague of crickets
    descending on a field of amaranth outside Teotihuacán
A thousand years before the Pacific wind made the same whine
    in the rigging of Cortéz's ships—so, buttocks tingling from the hard
Seat of her terrible chair, she watched young lawyers and entrepreneurs
    unconsciously at play on the volcanic plains of history and biology,
Creatures, as far as she could tell, devoid of language, their lips moving
    hungrily, and she thought of a film she'd seen about the Mariana Trench,
Subaqueous life forms crowding around volcanic vents like Arctic explorers
    around a tiny stove at the heart of the great dark ice sheet:
She and her friend—who was terribly late—had done the same things decades ago
    when they were lovers on another planet, where jazz leaked in
Through speakers in the magnificent paneling, even in the toilets,
    and they drank Manhattans and one another and everything made sense.

WILLOW

Sometimes the willow is immutable, and I don't know why,
     any more than I know why darkness travels
From midnight to midnight faster than thought. I spend
     part of every morning saying *I don't know* to the geranium
And part saying *I can't say* to the cat sleeping by the door.
     I'm trying to make up for the times I cannot bring myself
To admit my ignorance and I keep on talking, when the quarrel
     will not stop itself in my larynx. *Oh foolish language,*
Just be still, someone might beg, but it keeps on running
     like a cement mixer on steroids. You might as well say
Begone to the whirlwind, or will the garbage truck in the alley
     not to exist. The Logos gets me by the throat, the riptide
Of its endless sentence contradicting absence, canceling silence,
     dragging me down forever into the vortex of utterance.
It wants to outline how the blood cells flicker in sexual patterns,
     it wants to parse how the neutrino knows its nest.
I stand on the stump of the willow at high noon on a Tuesday,
     letting discourse immerse me. Even the dead are helpless
In its corrosive current. They keep muttering over and over,
     Bring us a bowl of goat's blood so we can suck it down
And argue. It's tradition. And if I mourn a little for the tree
     that shaded me even before sunrise, it goes on living surely
In the brackish plasma where the syllables hyphenate and breed.

NOBODY

Nobody knows the day or the hour, certainly not
    the crow in the black walnut down the block
Stealing bits of tinfoil perhaps to make a tiny hat
    to shield his tiny brain from tiny alien messages—
He is making a speech in Serbian, I think, and I'd take notes
    except he does not know the day or the hour,
Any more than the squirrel sitting on the curb outside
    the kitchen window working his pendulous cheeks and laughing
Probably at me, this moron who has gathered no discernable nuts
    and surely won't make it through the winter,
But the squirrel does not know the name of the nanosecond
    or what key it will assign my last stridulous breath—
I'd prefer D minor if I had a choice, it ought to be funereal—
    the squirrel can't even explain why we name the days
And the months but not the years, we skip from months
    straight to epochs, ages, and eras, and we could guess
The era or the epoch, but not the day or hour, nobody can, not even
    the spider, patient under the awning, waiting an age or three if she must
To enlighten the moth, the cricket, the ant, and most archetypally the fly.

WHITENESS

It's an ice storm, transparent and all-devouring.
    Who has power when the rain's weight hardens
Everywhere anything connects? No one can even walk
    without breaking bones, or looking like a clown.
So much for the neighborhood, locked in its pale sublime.
    At midday it blinds you, the oblivious sun
A purity so potent you cover your face and moan. I am
    one of them. I am there when even the trees break down,
Splinters of the state of nature jagged on the lawn.

LOST SOCK

I was trying to read St. John of the Cross,
    but my mind kept sliding off.
It would hit the floor, bounce like a cheap
    plastic mug, skitter under the sofa,
And come to rest among tumbleweeds
    of cat hair, a 1947 penny, the wool sock
I'd spent a whole week looking for. Beyond,
    near the wall, everything just went black.
My mind went there in the form of a vessel
    to fill itself with that measure of nothingness
And return to me humbly, so that I too could then return
    to *Dark Night of the Soul* bearing my own
Darkness, so that I could close my eyes and read
    and travel toward my spirit in the void,
Barefoot on the road of lacerating stones, one sock
    in my left hand crying out blind for the other.

ANGER MANAGEMENT

I was angry when the dog pulled my copy
    of *On the Genealogy of Morals* off the table
And chewed on it for half a day in the alcove
    before I found out. I managed to drag
One sentence out of his slathering jaws—
    Of necessity we remain strangers to ourselves—
And found the utterance uncharacteristically
    damp for Nietzsche. The rest of the book
Was inside the dog, and you know what that means:
    He had swallowed *We are noble, good, beautiful,*
and happy!—swallowed it whole, dumb mutt—
    and I knew I'd find it on the lawn in a day or two,
Alongside *Nothing is true, everything is permitted.*
    He was digesting that one at this very moment,
Thereby undoing four hundred dollars' worth
    of dog obedience class. I tell you I was furious.
It was my favorite book, I'd owned it for decades,
    its marginalia traced the history of my conscience.
But I coaxed him out of hiding, I gave him a cookie,
    I stroked his ears and went on reading Nietzsche
In my head (*Each one of us is farthest away from himself*).
    I could not punish a dog for only doing
The same thing I had done, but more quickly and completely.
    This satisfied Nietzsche, who scratched my belly,
Threw a ball across the room, and stood with his hand out, waiting.

GAZEHOUND

Resting on a park bench, I saw Plato
    walking—he was a borzoi on a glittering leash—
Across the footbridge toward the exit. My first
    thought was *Where on earth*
Did they get that dog? It had been four decades
    since I last saw a borzoi. That was in frozen
Montreal. I was young, of course, dreaming of lovers,
    of course, whose names I could not imagine
In the narrow suburbs of my medulla oblongata.
    Just then someone shouted *Plato!* at the dog,
And I was thinking how clever to call a dog that,
    when the owner shrieked *Ne pas chier*
Sur le trottoir! and yanked hard on the chain.
    Not a borzoi, a gazehound, *canis agasaeus*,
Adored by the ancient Greeks and had at great price.
    But these were French-shrieking lovers and the dog was theirs,
The woman held the chain in her hand, she was staring down a tunnel
    of light at a man slumped on a park bench smelling
Smoke, the stream beneath the footbridge engulfed in flame,
    and the bridge too, everything was burning, sulfurous fumes
Of recall rolling toward him over the grass in the shape of a man
    walking in flames, calmly adjusting his toga,
And from the other side of oblivion a chained animal howling.
    The great thing is not to care too much about one's own mind.
How pure can memory be? The borzoi wasn't Plato, it was
    Heraclitus, such a different philosopher, such an awkward name
To shout in the snow while yanking an ambiguous lead.

SOLITAIRE

There are worse things than being awake
     at four in the morning, but it would be
Too depressing to make a list, so I putter
     in the kitchen, wash last night's wineglasses,
Wipe down the counter, make a coffee.
     I try to read, but I don't have my reader's
Mind yet. I want to know more about the change
     from primary orality to literacy in ancient Greece,
But I don't become literate myself before 9 a.m.
     In the end I put down the book. I pick up
A deck of cards and lay out a game of solitaire.
     I lose four in a row, and by now I'm obsessed,
I lay the cards out again. If I'd just cheat a little—
     my grandmother always cheated, and took
The greatest pleasure in it—I could win and move on,
     but I don't. I have my principles. *Not life,*
But good life, is to be chiefly valued, Socrates is saying,
     but solitaire is a bitch of a game. I keep shuffling
And playing. No one is awake but me. Socrates
     didn't write: he *said* that. I can hear his whiny voice
Saying other things too, like *Practice music, eat your tzatziki,*
     drink your hemlock. Usually you play
Solitaire alone, but suddenly I am playing solitaire
     with death, at 4 a.m. Who isn't? *What the hell,*
Socrates says, *Cheat death a little. Everybody's doing it.*

HALO

It's a first world problem, I know, but today
    I woke up with a country-western song
Stuck in my head—not even a real one, a song
    I wrote in my sleep, and not even a whole one,
But just the chorus, which goes round and round
    in Merle Haggard's voice. Don't get me wrong—
I like Merle Haggard. But this sliver of music
    is driving me bat-shit crazy, it makes me want
To crawl through my own ear into my brain and find
    whatever sleazy bar these two songwriters
Are still hanging out in—I know in the marrow
    of my synapses there's a pair of them; they're swilling
Coors Lite and congratulating each other—and beat them
    songless with the neck of a 1932 Martin parlor guitar
That just happens to be lying there (my head is full of them).
    What were they thinking? I know you can get away
With a thousand clichés in any kind of music, but did they
    have to write *Some people are born to be golden/*
Some people are just born to fail? Why do I get *this*
    and not at least a jazz riff, or, better, a full requiem?
I forgave Merle Haggard years ago for "Okie from Muskogee."
    In the 60s I hated that, and him, but now I know him better.
Forgiveness of all kinds is still possible. Maybe
    I'll help these guys up, maybe I'll buy them a decent beer
And just beg them to revise. Maybe I'll walk out of the bar
    onto the boulevard of my amygdala, where young people
In love are actually sauntering. It looks like Paris here, or heaven,
    there ought to be a winged accordionist in a beret playing Piaf,
I should live in a place like this, and I would, but this song won't stop:
    If I grew a halo like an angel/ They'd run me out of town on a rail.

TINFOIL BOAT

after YK

There is trouble in the geranium, trouble
      in the microwave, trouble in the walls
Of the house. I have to travel to the other world
      to find I don't know what, not a decoder ring
Or a magic mandolin—I have to travel for nothing.
      Le voyage pour le voyage. Will nothing
Change this plague of shadows? I don't know.
      That's the problem with this problem.
I have forgotten the coordinates, I don't have
      a tinfoil boat that can navigate the æther,
I don't know songs that open ambrosial doors.
      The only mushrooms in the house
Are dried porcini, nice in pasta, no good for the journey.
      The dead are getting sleepy with impatience,
One is holding a stalk of wheat to bless me, one
      is cleaning a .38 revolver. I am sitting in my chair
Trying to fly to them, I have my hands against my chest,
      I am singing a song by Auden that doesn't release me,
Though I note with approval the genius of his rhyme.

CENTIPEDE

He is enormous and immediately repulsive,
    sailing down the wainscoting. I think of him
As *he* though I cannot verify the gender, knowing nothing
    of the intimate habits of arthropods. I place
A drinking glass over him tenderly. Magnified
    by the clear curve of the vessel, he reveals
Nothing at all except otherness, so in order to release him
    into the flower garden by the porch, I must decide
He is a ship, an oared Roman galley, bearing saffron
    for mindless patricians, propelled by slaves of the Empire,
And I am an admiral of Carthage. That done,
    we sign a treaty and he scuds away over tides
Of hostas, into the distant uncharted zone of banked
    gerbera daisies, revolting as I was when I set out
On Charon's boat, voyaging upward from the land of the dead,
    threading my course from petal to portal, from sill to joist to jamb.

HEXAGRAM WITH NO CHANGING LINES

This light, this rain, these maples
    through the mist: something is coming apart
In the mountain. I say *armadillo* to the wind-rasp, *rat* to the color
    of the leaves. Why shouldn't earth be my medium? But I am
Stuck in a locust's shell shredding in the weather, a shimmer
    of oil in the street. Decorum. I haven't been dead very long.

SNAIL

I draw a snail for my daughters, because I can.
    Anyone can draw a snail. The easy thing
Is the shell, a simple spiral. Harder is the face,
    which looks at my daughters with my eyes
And they see there all the snail sees: so much breakage
    down where he lives among the clods and potsherds,
Crumbs of colored glass, sticks, stalks, deconstructed stone,
    and—crushed by pigeons and scattered in a compost
Of Carthaginian salt—bits of shell the others left behind.

SALT

About ancient Carthage I know almost nothing
    except how it ended. Where people went on a Tuesday,
What they ate for dinner: blank. But Scipio Africanus the Younger,
    the siege, the burning forum, the soldiers with their sacks
Of salt: indelible in my memory. I might as well have been there.
    I can say the same about the retired machinist, a stranger
From two blocks over who died mowing his lawn: the sirens
    on a Saturday, the flashing lights, the curious neighbors mumbling.
Would Roman soldiers have carried salt in bags or barrels?
    How far, and at how great an expense? Probably never happened.
Carthage does live on as a suburb, and for a week or so I might
    pass that stranger's house and still be able to think *Nice lawn.*

VULTURE

I can still see the imperious vulture etched
    on the back wall of my mind's cave,
Where he came to be when I witnessed him exit
    the belly of a dead cow collapsed
Like a suburb of ancient Troy in the shade
    of a black cedar. He came forth, a shining priest,
From the temple of the dead, settling his wings
    around him—sacramental robes, I might
Have thought if I had not been myself
    ignorant as the swarm of vestal flies
Attending him, lighting on his raiment
    to lick him clean. He had worshiped
Under the white dome of the cow's ribcage,
    he had prayed as he had learned to pray:
All-devouringly, indifferent to the ants
    and carrion beetles swarming at his feet,
Exulting in the incense of his sacrifice.
    I was a child, indifferent to the ways
The dead deal with the dead until he turned
    his hieratic head and regarded me,
Considering my bitter self-taste at his leisure
    before he flexed and rose and drove himself
Through my eyes' barrier to become indelible
    in the heretofore godless arc of my interior sky.

BELOVED

I was looking for something and had even forgotten
    what it was, exactly, except I needed it—
This was like a dream scenario, but I was all too awake,
    ransacking the house like a starving ferret,
Looking in drawers, under stacks of books, behind
    the refrigerator, which isn't easy to do. I did
Find an earring, and thirty-four cents, a useful sum.
    I found a toy soldier. I had no idea where it came from—
A mercenary from a foreign army, scouting out the house.
    It was like enlightenment, always almost in reach,
Always on the edge of my brain, hovering like a dragonfly,
    or the sword of Damocles, but I could no more call it forth
Than I could find it under a pile of junk mail,
    or in the corner on the far side of the piano,
Until my wife, wondering what all the noise was, appeared
    in front of me, took one look, and just said *Here.*

FOSSILS

We sat at dinner talking of the usual small turmoils
    of the day—work, weather, children,
Money, politics (how on earth *could* they?)—
    and as we talked, the pneumatic sacs in our chests
Pushed air, our larynxes sang in that wind
    like Aeolian harps, and who knows what went on
In our brains. Where did the words come from?
    How many mouths had they passed through,
What did they mean in the 14th century, how did they sound
    in the sewers of London, in the stinking holds
Of slave ships, in Chaucer's inner ear? *Language*
    is fossil poetry, wrote Emerson, ossifying as he wrote.
We sat at dinner spitting fossils across the tablecloth,
    pinging each other with history, oblivious, still in love.

CONSTITUTIONAL

A block and a half down the hill to town, there's a threshold
    where darkness tilts to light, an axis that defines
The seasons of sorrow and joy. Every day I walk there to see
    what it means to my personal weather. Farther on
There's a coffee shop and a newsstand; then the shadowy shaft
    of a tunnel under the tracks to the depot. Then the river.
Sometimes there's a sailboat wrestling the current, flapping
    its blinding sails. Sometimes there's a barge of gray cargo.
I go there too, sipping the steam off a latte, eating a pastry,
    reading the headlines with the usual detached despair,
But that crack in the pavement in front of the yellow cottage
    with a concrete deer on the lawn—do humans live there,
Or only a couple of gnomes and a plastic frog?—marks the place
    where the black squirrel, crossing the meridian, turned albino.
I saw this happen. And a raven flying over became a saccharine dove.
    Every time I cross, I pause to add up my losses and count the change
In the pocket of my psyche. I'll need every dime for a ticket
    on the homely ferry that will drift me back from the inhuman
Forested shore to the wharf with lanterns hung from posts
    weathered to the color of fossilized bone, past the Calvinists
And the town hall's bipolar flag and the little park where two dirty boys
    are playing marbles, gambling their allowance that there is
In fact such a thing in the world as winning, to the blue house
    where all I love is getting on with things the way real people do
When they're done with metamorphosis, and know exactly who they are.

ANTIQUITIES

Slowly up the frozen slope, wheezing
　　like a ruptured yak, I make my way
To the viewpoint above our ice-choked river.
　　A fogbank has risen over the mountain
On the far side, but the morning sun burns
　　everything down. The river's surface glows.
I assume the posture I saw an old Tibetan take
　　in a painting, propped against a rock face, resting
For the final flight. It's not so bad being ancient.
　　Ask the wind-smoothed boulder. Ask the fogbank.
Ask the moon, the next time you see her
　　admiring herself in water: her pitted face
Is the price of enlightenment. Ask the river.
　　The old painters loved how the air here filled
With the aura of diffusion, how distance softened
　　the blow. I lay my hand on the granite, cold
As any headstone. I don't mind joining the old ones,
　　leaning like that ancient sycamore, groaning like the Hudson
When it grinds away the moments, floe against floe.

LETTER TO HERACLITUS

I've been thinking about you a lot, and I'm onto you.
    There was never a manuscript. There was never a body
Of writing, lovely and coherent, that you could give your wife
    for Ancient Greek Christmas, my favorite holiday,
And she would open it and see that you'd dedicated it to her
    and she'd cry and you'd have great sex. If it had existed
It would have been a scroll, of course, made of papyrus
    shipped all the way from Egypt. Very pricey. Nice gift.
Never happened. Those little bits of Heraclitus you can find
    scattered all over the library were always just that: little bits.
Here's one now: *Not knowing how to listen, they know not*
    how to speak. Not a word in there about writing.
You didn't publish. You perished. That's why you're not around
    to clean up the mess you made. The brilliant, glorious mess.

AS FOR ENLIGHTENMENT

I mean it in the sense of *a state of consciousness*,
    not as in *The 18th Century*, although I wouldn't mind
Being Voltaire for a day. When I hear Buddhists
    discoursing, it seems impossible, as if
It would take decades of meditation and a diet
    of pure tofu to attain, but they also say
It's easy, it's already there, and I know they're right.
    I am an enlightened being, when I remember
I am one. Sort of. So are you. It's like stepping over the threshold
    of a room where a splendid party is going on, but everyone's
A stranger—you can't go in and mingle, they'd notice you
    and summon a ferocious gendarme with brass knuckles
And a knife—so you just stand there, inches inside, not moving.
    You feel sentience flow through you like the river of Heraclitus.
You are paralyzed with embarrassment, but shining.

PLAYLIST

When the end comes, let there be a killer
    soundtrack, a susurrus of reeds, real ones
Blown in the wind by the river, let the voice
    of the river be in it, and the rumble of stones
Rolling down the mountain forever. For me
    let it come on an Easter Sunday. Just as Jesus
Shoulders back the sweating stone, I will slip inside
    and go out where he came in, with a choir
Of falcons attendant, soaring raptor harmonies,
    and a vulture conducting. Let there be more
Overdubs than any engineer could fathom,
    every molecule of my being leaving its sonic trace
In that liminal zone to which the resurrected commute,
    headphones on, tuned in to the playlist of my passing.

THE FLOWER AT THE END OF
THE WORLD

Immortal mortals, mortal immortals, one living the other's death
and dying the other's life.
     —HERACLITUS

It was a 1954 Ford pickup truck that stopped
    on the shoulder of the road in front of me.
The driver leaned over and popped open the door
    as I trotted up. Getting in, I looked him over,
A big man with long silver hair and a cowboy hat,
    and I knew him at once as Heraclitus disguised
As a Mongolian shaman of the Buryat people. *Where*
    you heading? he asked. *End of the world,* I said.
He nodded. *Not surprised. I'm heading there myself.*

*

Next a hooded rat guided me through a tunnel
    every available surface of which—walls,
Floor, ceiling—held a door. There were hundreds,
    perhaps millions, of every shape and size.
I traveled the shaft for hours, walking on jambs,
    bumping into lintels, tripping on knobs and latches,
The rat scampering ahead of me. I struggled
    not to step on his hideous tail. At last he stopped
And scratched on a door set in the wall. *How do you know,*
    I asked him, *that it's this one?* He squinted at me
In disgust. *It has your name all over it,* he said. *Can't you read?*

*

Then I was back in my second-grade classroom
        doing a timed reading test. I opened the book
And nothing I saw made sense. *The rat was right,*
        I thought. *I* can't *read.* But just then the teacher,
Kindly Mrs. Mullins—I was her pet—came to me,
        draped me in a black cape, led me to the back
Of the room to the science table, and locked me in my cage.

*

But the timer kept ticking. I was failing the test.
        I would become a laughingstock, be thrown
Out of school, make a life in a cardboard box
        under an overpass. My cage *was* a cardboard box,
The traffic was thundering above me, I had a crust
        of sandwich dug from a dumpster, I had a grimy robe
St. Francis gave me. St. Francis sat next to me,
        his back against the abutment. He was covered in birds.
Listen, kid, he said in a ratlike voice, *the secret of life*
        is a secret. Stop worrying. All of us are homeless bums.

*

At the shelter, they gave me a bowl of soup, a map,
        and a set of car keys. It was a pleasure
To have a Mercedes, but the map was a treasure,
        there were instructions in a pirate's scrawl
And at the center an X. You'd think the end of the world
        would be that obvious. The problem is, the road
Is your life, and your life is a secret. I drove
        for hours on the Autobahn, the Mercedes
Was a dream. It felt like oblivion on wheels.
        I could drive this way forever.

*

Listen, the rat said. He turned up at the crucial moment
    I was struggling to change a flat tire. *You're a moron.*
You'll never get there this way. Take the short cut.
    There was a naked path by the highway
Leading into a littered bog. *What do you think?* I asked.
    St. Francis shrugged. *Six of one*, he said.
So I left the car teetering on its jack, and headed
    out through the sumac and muddy beer cans.
The rat waved its tail. *Turn left*, St. Francis said,
    when you get to the middle of nowhere.

*

The middle of nowhere is an X.
    It's a clearing in the middle of a forest,
Midway of course in life's journey of course,
    where vultures circle. I watched them a while—
They were a great grim dance in a grim gray sky—
    and meditated a little. Maybe I prayed a little.
I'm not sure what the difference is. When I turned
    left, I was in a whipped-out trailer park.

*

Everything was abandoned, the cheap mobile homes,
    the swing sets and sandboxes, the folding chairs,
A dented blue tricycle lying on its side, one wheel turning.
    I walked up and down the rows, all the trailers alike,
Windows broken out, axles rusting. When I turned a corner,
    I saw him sitting on a camp stool. His cowboy hat

Had a gold medallion on the crown, and he wore
    a bolo tie with a turquoise clasp. *So you finally got here,*
He said, and he pointed at the last trailer, which bore a banner,
    blue, with gold lettering: *Welcome to the end of the world.*

*

The trailer was clean and empty except for a wooden table
    by the window. Someone had set a shallow dish
With a jonquil growing in rocks and water, its bulb bare
    the way people force them to bloom indoors.
It had been there a little overlong, its three white blossoms
    browning at the edges, and the foliage
Sickly and limp. I got some water from the sink
    but I knew it was futile. The timer was ticking,
The test was going on, and the flowers had the faces
    of my wife and daughters—I could see them clearly there
At a great distance, fading from me, but the perfume
    of the jonquil was oddly like an orchid, or a poppy,
Or a black rose, and St. Francis was saying, *You should have paid
    more attention to the birds,* and the rat was saying,
Humans make such a big deal of it, and Heraclitus
    said nothing. He pointed, standing by the open door.

AFTER THE AFTERLIFE

Wherever I return, it won't be Paris,
    though it will probably be raining,
A late afternoon in February when everyone
    is in despair. Eternity will have passed
In seconds, a brief blackout like a hot
    seizure in the brain. A fogbank
Is rolling in off the river. Cannons fire
    from invisible ships: they are looking
For the drowned man, but he is clever,
    his death is a cloak, and he is hidden
In the labyrinth of his own impervious dreaming.
    I reappear at a table on the sidewalk
Outside a small café, under a torn umbrella,
    just as an empty plate is set
On the cloth before me. My dripping hands
    leave their muddy imprints
On the napkin as I unfold it. It seems
    the river has followed me. The last thing
I remember was talking to Vallejo. He was sitting
    right here, just a moment ago. But now
The evening darkens, and the fog shrinks
    the valley to a single streetlight over
What used to be the dock, where a black boat
    rocks in the wake of everything that is passing.
What did I order? What do they use in this place
    to pay the bill? Will I have to sign my name?
I can hold a pen with only bones for hands, but who
    will I say is writing in the blank where I should be?

ACKNOWLEDGMENTS

The author gratefully acknowledges publication in the following magazines:

Blackbird, Cutthroat, Hinchas de Poesia, Inertia, The Kenyon Review, The New Yorker, Plume, Poetry South, Poet's Country.

"Minutae" was reprinted in *The Best American Poetry 2016.*